NUMBER'S MAGIC

A GUIDE TO NUMEROLOGY

SHALU SINGH

TO ALL SEEKERS OF HIDDEN TRUTHS AND EXPLORERS OF THE UNSEEN REALMS. MAY YOUR JOURNEY INTO THE OCCULT SCIENCES BE FILLED WITH ENLIGHTENMENT, WISDOM AND DISCOVERY OF THE MYSTERIES THAT LIE BEYOND THE VEIL.

Contents

Foreword

Numerology, the ancient study of the mystical significance of numbers, has fascinated scholars, mystics, and seekers of truth for centuries. In a world that often feels governed by chaos and randomness, numerology offers a sense of order, revealing patterns and meanings that lie beneath the surface of our everyday lives.

This book delves deep into the art and science of numerology, unraveling the secrets of numbers and their profound impact on our destinies. Whether you are a seasoned practitioner or a curious newcomer, you will find a wealth of knowledge and insights within these pages.

The author, Shalu Singh, brings a unique blend of expertise, passion, and intuition to this work. With years of study and practical experience, she has crafted a comprehensive guide that is both accessible and profound. Her ability to distill complex concepts into clear, understandable language makes this book an invaluable resource for anyone interested in exploring the world of numerology.

In Number's Magic, you will discover the meanings of individual numbers, the significance of number combinations, and how to calculate and interpret your own numerological chart. The author also explores the historical and cultural contexts of numerology, providing a rich tapestry of knowledge that connects the ancient past with the present day.

As you embark on this journey, I encourage you to keep an open mind and a receptive heart. Numerology is not just a tool for prediction but a pathway to greater self-awareness and understanding. It offers insights into our personalities, life paths, and potential challenges, guiding us toward a more harmonious and fulfilling existence.

May this book be your guide and companion as you explore the fascinating world of numerology. May it inspire you to see the hidden patterns in your life and to harness the power of numbers to unlock your true potential.

Welcome to the world of numerology. Your journey of discovery begins now.

Preface

Numerology, the ancient study of numbers and their mystical meanings, has captivated the human imagination for millennia. From the pyramids of Egypt to the temples of India, cultures across the globe have sought to understand the hidden significance of numbers in shaping our destinies. As a bridge between the tangible and the spiritual, numerology offers profound insights into our personalities, life paths, and the universe's grand design.

This book is a journey into the fascinating world of numerology, where numbers are not just symbols, but living entities that influence our lives in ways we might never have imagined. Whether you are a curious beginner or a seasoned practitioner, this guide aims to provide you with a comprehensive understanding of numerology's principles and applications.

Throughout these pages, you will explore the foundational concepts of numerology, including the meanings of the core numbers, the significance of your birth date, and how to calculate and interpret your Personality Number. Each chapter is designed to build your knowledge step by step, empowering you to uncover the unique numeric blueprint that shapes your life's journey.

In a world often dominated by logic and reason, numerology offers a refreshing perspective that honors intuition, synchronicity, and the mysterious ways the universe communicates with us. By understanding the vibrational essence of numbers, we can gain clarity, find purpose, and make more informed decisions that align with our true selves.

As you embark on this numerological exploration, I encourage you to keep an open mind and heart. Allow the wisdom of the numbers to guide you, illuminate your path, and reveal the deeper truths about who you are and what you are here to accomplish. May this book be a valuable companion on your journey of self-discovery and spiritual growth.

Welcome to the enchanting realm of numerology. Let the numbers speak.

Shalu Singh

Acknowledgements

Writing a book is a journey that is never undertaken alone, and I am deeply grateful to the many people who have supported me along the way.

First and foremost, I would like to thank Dr. Rohit Gadkari for their unwavering support and encouragement. Your belief in me and my work has been a constant source of inspiration. It is because of that this book has now been brought to light.

A special thanks to my husband and my children for their patience, understanding, and love during the countless hours I spent writing and researching. Your support has made all the difference.

I am also grateful to [publisher] for believing in this project and providing the necessary guidance and resources to bring it to fruition. Your professional expertise and commitment have been instrumental in shaping this book.

To my colleagues and peers in the space of numerology, thank you for your constructive feedback and stimulating discussions. Your input has been invaluable in refining my ideas and enhancing the quality of this work. Your constant help in decoding the contents of this book, helping me research the facts has been invaluable.

With gratitude,
Shalu Singh

CHAPTER ONE

INTRODUCTION TO NUMEROLOGY

Welcome to the magical world of decoding your birth numbers by yourself. The template of a person's life is written in their date of birth. Various dimensions of these numbers have been analyzed for decades for understanding of one's own nature in detail and to know in advance what life holds for them. Each person has a set of numbers that upon deciphering, determine their destiny, karmic, spiritual, emotional and personality influences.

The way our lives unfold is a pattern of cause and effect and when we knowingly perform a mental and action karma, we can design out own destiny and live a self-created fulfilling life.

Numerology is a self-help tool. Derived from Latin words "Numeros" meaning numbers and "logos" meaning science of study of, numerology simply means science and study of numbers.

It is a method of character analysis that uses date of birth to answer the eternal question of a human – "WHO AM I?"

Numerology is a branch of knowledge which deals with calculations and implications of numbers. It is a simple logical and accurate predictable since. Numbers have a relationship with living things and their energies, as it has been established over the centuries.

Numerology says that numbers have an impact on relationships, health, career, marriage, self-growth, success and many other areas of their lives.

To attain peace and happiness, a perfect balance of numbers is necessary. In numerology, every number has its own meaning and importance. It brings out the essence of life in the form of numbers starting from 1 to 9. These numbers have a lot of energy and positivity, each with its own traits, characteristics and strength. Based on birth dates, one can calculate their life path number and check their personality traits, characteristics, career, love and relationships.

Now the question arises on how to calculate Personality Number and Destiny Number.

Personality Number (P) describes your personality and nature and is calculated from your birth date. For example, date of birth of a person is 10-04-1991. So, the personality number becomes 1+0=1. Another example, date of birth of a person is 24-3-1981. So, the personality number becomes 2+4=6.

Destiny Number (D) talks about your destiny or life path, or in other words the direction you will go in your life. It is the total of all digits of your birth date. For example, date of birth of person is 10-04-1991. So, destiny number becomes 1+0+0+4+1+9+9+1=25. Now both digits are added together so, 2+5=7. Hence, destiny number is 7. Another example, date of birth is 24-3-1981. So, destiny number is 2+4+3+1+9+8+1=28. Now both these digits are added so 2+8=10. Both these digits are added again so 1+0=1. Hence the destiny number is 1.

CHAPTER TWO

PERSONALITY NUMBER 1

People born on 1. 10, 19 or 28 of any month have personality number 1.

- _Correlation with Astrology_

Personality number 1 is ruled by sun, which is the strongest planet according to astrology. Sun is the king of all planets, according to astrology. Life on earth is because of sun. The planetary influence of sun is majorly on the jaw line of a person. If the influence of sun is immense, the jawline would be strong and broad, forehead would be broad as well with receding hairline.

Person would be active, ready to help other in need. Since ruled by the Sun, people with P=1 live life king size. Also, if infected with any disease, the person would recover their health quickly. Sun also influences the person's life by making them fearless, providing them with pride in their position (both in personal life as well as professional life), fame, generosity, self-confidence, prestige and virtue.

- _General Description_

People with P=1 are good in sports and love physical activities and adventure. They are constantly trying to learn new things and hence have a variety of hobbies and skills. These people also love travelling as well as going on long drives alone or with their loved ones. They are also foody – they have a diverse palate and love cooking as well as trying out new kinds of dishes from different regions of the world.

- *Leaders*

These people are natural born leaders. They have great leadership qualities and have an authoritative nature. A good leader is anyone who is greatly aware of their strengths and weaknesses, their emotions, their thought process and their reactions to certain situations. They also garner great credibility for themselves throughout their life by focusing on relationship-building, exhibiting humility towards others, staying authentic and transparent, presenting themselves constantly and consistently and eventually become role models.

For example, a person with P=1 in a highly frustrating situation in a professional setting without fruitful outcomes would probably take a few moments to articulate their thoughts and emotions before guiding their team, creating a plan of action and eventually instructing their team members towards their goal.

- *Management Skills*

These people have great time management skills. Along with being punctual and disciplined, these people have control over the way they work, live or behave. They are extremely goal oriented and have a tendency to notice the finer details that might be missed by other people.

- *Interpersonal Relationships*

These people have strong communication skills and are active listeners. Being emotionally intelligent, they are able to control their emotions and have a calm aura around themselves, which is highly appreciated by their partners. They bring a positive aura to the relationship, being careful with their partner's feelings and inspiring and motivating them to achieve their goals as well. They are kind, generous and always put their partners first.

Also, these people usually have a very big friend circle. This is because they have such a positive outlook on life that people are attracted towards them and always want to befriend them. People with P=1 always accommodate more and more people in their life regardless of their age.

- *Advisor*

Through their vast experience, people with P=1 usually are able to guide and advice people through tough situations, challenges and help them find light even in the most testing times. Again, since they have such a positive attitude and outlook towards life, they are able to give solutions to those in need. They are always level-headed and always know when and how to talk to people to show them the right direction.

- *Hard Worker*

A person with P=1 is a very hard working person. A hard worker is someone who puts in much time and effort into their tasks and goals, regardless of the fact if it is personal or professional. They are dedicated, diligent, and committed towards putting a significant amount of effort and time towards their responsibilities.

However, such people should also realize that they might face a lot of failure before finally getting rewarded for their hard work. Everyone in life wants success but do not necessarily want the pain associated with repeatedly being rejected.

This is also where people with P=1 have an upper hand – they have a positive outlook on life. Of course, they face challenges and difficult situations and rejections before getting the reward, but they also realize that all their hard work will not go to waste. They have enough self-awareness and self-confidence to know that one day they would succeed and because of this positive attitude, they are able to overcome all the challenges and heartbreaks.

- _Workaholic_

Though being workaholic may positively affect their professional life, these people should also realize that they have to take time out for their friends and family. Having tight schedules with no proper vacations days or breaks may cause rifts and fights between their loved ones. To avoid this, people with P=1 must take out time for friends and family, take days off for self care, take vacation days and overall keep in mind that having a good work-life balance is also a key to happy, successful life.

- _Impressive Personality_

As someone who is successful and confident with great self awareness, people with P=1 usually come off as charming, someone with a very impressive personality. Through their ability to stay calm, to control their emotions in any situation, and by being kind and generous, their overall positive aura stands out in a crowd. Through conversations, other people might realize that people with P=1 have a positive outlook towards life and are able to see the best in people even when they are going through a rough patch in life.

This type of personality is greatly appreciated by their life partners as well as in a professional setting for the team. Not only does it allow for interpersonal relationships to nurture in a healthy way, but in a professional setting, it helps the team members discuss any situation with leaders with P=1 easily and in hopes of finding solutions.

- *Loyalty*

Loyalty means being their for someone through the highs and lows and staying by their side regardless of circumstances. People with P=1 are extremely loyal towards their family and the company they work for.

- *Self-made Person*

People with P=1 work with their own techniques and strongly believe in the motto, "my life, my rules". They are self-built people, having an origin supported by unquestionable evidence. They are authentic and do not like to copy other person's work. They complete their tasks in a way that is new and different from others.

- *Arrogant*

Arrogance is basically showing an offensive attitude of superiority. Since they are self made, people with P=1 often have a superiority complex and show off their worldly possessions. They give themselves the highest level of self importance, acting entitled to certain luxuries and behaving as if they are above everyone else. They act as if they know more than other people and their unpleasantly proud behavior may sometimes cause hostile environment around them, either within personal life or professional life. Such a behavior negatively affects people with P=1 since generally working or being around such people drains one's energy. Hence, sometimes people with P=1 are considered "energy vampires", i.e, it is exhausting to be around them and listening to how far they've come in life when they do not realize other people have different definitions of success.

- _Egoistic_

People with P=1 are self-centered, preoccupied with oneself and crave gratification of their own desires. They are absorbed in their own desires, thoughts and activities so much so at times that they expect everyone around them to also follow their principles and morals.

CHAPTER THREE

PERSONALITY NUMBER 2

People born on 2, 11, 20 or 29 of any month have personality number 2.

- *Correlation with Astrology*

Personality number 2 is governed by the moon and hence people with personality number 2 are often sensitive. Moon, according to astrology, influence hypothalamus, a part of brain responsible for all types of emotions. Influences of the Moon on face, according to astrology, is observed if the person has a round face with slight chubbiness. They also have big eyes. Other influences on the body include having a lower body temperature and being extremely lethargic and hence, others may consider them "lazy". These people don't have stable thought process. People with P=2 love eating sweet food stuff like chocolates, sweets, candies etc as well as milk and milk products. Such people are brutally honest, affectionate and have a positive outlook towards other people and life in general.

- *General Description*

One trait observed in people with P=2 is that they can never say 'no' to anyone, which might lead to them getting into arguments when others say no to them. It might also turn into a situation where others take advantage of them. This causes much heartbreak for people with P=2 since they expect everyone to act the way they do, which is with kindness. They love cleanliness and always keep their surrounding neat and well-organized. May have an interest in gardening, music as well as arts and crafts. A positive trait of people with P=2 is that they never get jealous, they are such happy-go-lucky people that they genuinely get happy for the success others achieve without getting jealous, strongly believing that they themselves would get success when they deserve it. Being emotionally stable, they realize that admitting there is something wrong and working towards getting it right and fixing it before it gets worse is another trait of people with P=2. This comes in handy when they have medical/health related issues since they do not allow their disease to worsen and get treatment in early stages itself. Also, since governed by the moon, people with P=2 might have issues sleeping during full moon and get easily irritated.

- _Sensitive_

People with P=2 get easily upset by things other think and say about them. They are extremely empathetic, and hence are kind, caring, able to pick up on the feelings of others and are aware of their needs and behaving in a way that helps them feel good. Since they are kind and caring, sometimes they do not understand how others could say cruel things or do unappreciable things to them, leading them to take everything personally.

- _Magnetic aura_

People with P=2 possess qualities or characteristics that make them appealing, intriguing or influential to others. They are charming, have a positive energy and draw others towards them effortlessly. It may be the way they maintain themselves, or the fact that they meticulously ensure to listen to the person in front of them and make them feel included in a group setting, but that is what makes them so attractive to others.

• _Emotional_

They are empathetic and hence are in great touch with their own emotions as well as of others. Emotions are intense feelings that are directed at someone or something. A positive or negative experience that is associated with a particular pattern of psychological activity may evoke certain emotions in people. Since people with P=2 are highly emotionally intelligent, they are able to regulate their emotions in very extensive ways, and also help others do the same.

• _Soft spoken_

They usually have a gentle, quiet voice and mannerisms. People with P=2, in general with a large group, have the most soothing effect over others due to this and hence can be quiet popular. They do have strong opinions that they put forward but do so in a calm manner.

• _Supportive nature_

They are consistently helpful and encouraging to others. They help and support anyone in a difficult situation and try to make those unhappy, happy. They may do so by distracting the unhappy ones, taking them out on shopping sprees or out in the park etc. they also might give some good advice if they have past experience with similar situations, but are most importantly helpful in helping others regulate and understand their emotions better.

• _Family oriented_

Being close to family members and supporting them in their endeavors is extremely important to people with P=2. They are always willing to lend a helping hand, more so with family members since they give the utmost importance to blood relations. People with P=2 give major priority to their blood relatives and hence put their needs before their own. They take care of their family in their bad times and also are willing to give them everything, from monetary support to emotional support. They do not expect anything in return and truly believe in supporting family till the end. This may sometimes lead to fights between members, hostility amongst immediate family etc., since people with P=2 do not know where the limit is. It may make few family members take advantage of their kindness and being emotional and sensitive, people with P=2 may also end up being the doormat for others.

- *<u>Physical and Emotional Strength</u>*

People with P=2 may not be physically strong but are mentally and emotionally extremely stable. With special emphasis on people born on 11th of any month not being physically strong, it does not mean that they cant do basic weight lifting, but they lack stamina. If told to run a marathon or carry heavy bags for a long period of time, people with P=2 may not be able to do so due to lack of stamina. This is of course, not to say that they cant build their stamina or they cant improve their physical strength, but it takes longer for them to do so than other people.

- *<u>Partnership</u>*

Partnership is an arrangement between two or more people to oversee business operations. In a firm, people with P=2 contribute something, whether it be ideas, property, money or a combination of these. In a group of people handling a particular project, people with P=2 ensure that their team members have every resource they can provide to reach their goal.

- *"Flickering" nature*

Flickering here refers to that of a candle. People with P=2 have very irregular movements, and are very unsteady by their nature. Similar to a candle flickering with the wind, which fluctuates light, people with P=2 shine bright like a burning star or dim down like a dying star.

- *Mood swings*

A sudden or intense change in a person's emotional state. During a mood swing, an individual may quickly switch from feeling happy to feeling sad, irritable or angry. For example, a person with P=2 preparing for a difficult entrance exam. That person may go through phases of high motivation and determination to prepare well for their exam, but may also have moments of doubt and anxiety. This, paired with pressure from family, peers and the society may make them lash out at their close ones, may make them frustrated or demotivated etc.

- *Need for motivation*

People with P=2 usually require motivation from their close ones during challenging times. This is especially important for them since they choose to cut people off based on who supports them during difficult times and who doesn't. Since they are there for others, they expect the same from others as well. Motivation can be for any situation, be it motivation for studying for an entrance, or to fix their relationships. It becomes pertinent for others to support and motivate people with P=2 as well since people with P=2 are extremely emotional and may take wrong actions or speak the wrong things that they don't even mean.

- *Good hosts*

A person who invites guests to his/her home etc and provides them with food, drinks etc. being a good host, however, does not only mean providing rounds and rounds of food and drinks. People with P=2 create a welcoming atmosphere by having their space clean and organized, they offer refreshments based on their guest's preferences and dietary restrictions, be attentive by initiating and participating in conversations and making everyone feel included etc. they also plan activities or arrange for entertainment to keep the atmosphere lively, engaging and heart warming. At the end, people with P=2 express their gratitude for their guest's presence.

- *Intuitive*

Feeling or understanding that makes you believe or know that something is true without being able to explain why. Direct perception of truth, fact etc., independent of any reasoning process, immediate apprehension. For example, a person with P=2 is walking home with a few of their friends during night. As they approach a dimly lit alley, an unease washes over on person with P=2 and quickly asks their friends to move to a different route trusting her intuition. Different situations may occur, where people with P=2 might guess something out of the blue, like the place they're out to dinner, or guessing a person's call just before their phone rings etc. They might mistaken it for coincidence and just one sentence for you – too many coincidences make a pattern.

- *Sharp memory*

Rapidity, length of time, accuracy of recall or recognition and serviceableness. People with P=2 remember things very well. This may manifest as remembering small thing and recalling it several days, months or sometimes even years later. People with P=2 grasp and retain complex concepts easily, remember names and faces od people they've met, learn new things quickly and retain the knowledge effectively and their memory performance is persistent over time. They may also pay close attention to details in their surroundings, indicating an active and observing mind. They are also able to make connections between pieces of information easily, just like any good detective would.

PERSONALITY NUMBER 3

People born on 3, 12, 21 or 30 of any month have personality number 3.

- *Correlation with astrology*

People with P=3 are governed by Jupiter. Influences of Jupiter on the face can be seen as people with P=3 would have slight pale, yellow undertones or have brown complexion. With the hair as well, these people will have pale yellow hair or have brown hair. Also, their hair density would be thin to extremely thin. People with P=3 may have strong physique however, may be either a bit lethargic or active. People with P=3 are influences by Jupiter since they mature before their age and are quiet "serious" from their childhood. These people also have a tendency to gain weight. They are major foodies as well. If the influences of "guru", according to astrology are positive, then the person would feel extremely ambitious to learn new things, skills etc. they would actively seek new knowledge. Moreover, if the influences are positive then the person would also be loved by the elderly people. It also makes the person honest, liberal, loyal, religious, honest etc.

- *General description*

Such people are good in studies since they are extremely knowledge hungry and they would do extremely well in teaching line since they explain concepts in detail and easy-to-understand language. They are punctual and often are irritated if others aren't. They like their tasks done at a particular time. Whatever field they enter in, they try their best to achieve wonders in that particular field. Being knowledge seekers, they try their best to know everything in their subjects and hence, they excel in those fields as well. They might not like legal cases if they are a part of it.

- *Knowledge seekers*

A state in which one wants to learn more about something, "Seeker" here refers to the intensity or quantity of something one wants to gain. Some signs that may indicate their knowledge seeking behavior include curiosity, inquisitiveness, open-mindedness, curious learning, critical thinking, passion for discovery etc. they are adaptable, they have problem-solving skills and are self motivating. They try to grasp at new opportunities to learn and gain more knowledge, whether it be a summer school or staying in the library to read the new book added.

- *Occult sciences*

Occult sciences was used in the 16th century to refer to astrology, alchemy and natural magic. Various theories and practices involving a belief in a knowledge or use of supernatural forces or beings. While the term occult carries connotations of secrecy or mysticism, it can cover a wide range of subjects such as astrology, alchemy, spiritualism, parapsychology, numerology etc.

- *Creative*

Being creative means having or showing an ability to make new things or think of new ideas. They are willing to explore new ideas, perspectives and possibilities and are also receptive to unconventional ways of thinking. They display a strong desire to learn and explore new topics, interests and experiences, often asking though-provoking questions and seeking out diverse sources of inspiration. They express unique and innovative viewpoints, approaches and interpretations, demonstrating an individualistic style and creative voice.

- *<u>Leaders</u>*

Leaders have a set of qualities necessary to lead people or an organization. Leadership is the skill of motivation, guiding and inspiring people to work together towards a common goal. An effective leader has characteristics such as self confidence, strong communication and management skills, creative and innovative thinking. They demonstrate a clear vision for the future and set ambitious yet achievable goals. They display self assurance and conviction in their decisions and actions, instilling confidence in others and earning their trust and respect. They communicate effectively and persuasively, articulating ideas, goals and expectations clearly and inspiring others to take action through compelling messaging.

- *<u>Patient</u>*

The ability of being able to stay calm and not get angry, especially when there is a difficulty or you have to wait a long time. The ability to accept delay, suffering or annoyance without complaining. They engage in mindfulness meditation to cultivate present-moment awareness and observe their thoughts and emotions without judgement. The recognize that some things take time to unfold or achieve. They set realistic goals and expectations for yourself and others, and acknowledge that progress may be gradual. They put themselves in the shoes of others and try to understand their perspectives and experiences. Cultivating empathy helps them develop greater patience and compassion in their interactions with others.

- *Rule and regulation follower*

Rules are specific guidelines or instructions created by an organization or authority to regulate behavior and activities. Regulations are official rules and directions established by the government or regulatory body, typically with legal bindings, to govern specific sectors or industries. Although being a rules and regulation follower is a positive trait, it may sometimes cause issues. For example, Alice, a diligent employee committed to following company rules, faced a dilemma when a critical report for an important client meeting was incomplete due to a glitch in the new software system. Despite knowing the old system could generate the report immediately, she adhered strictly to the policy prohibiting its use and waited for IT to fix the issue, causing the report to be unavailable during the meeting. This led to client dissatisfaction and potential revenue loss. Alice's rigid adherence to rules, though usually a strength, highlighted the need for flexibility and pragmatic decision-making in urgent situations.

- *Punctual*

They like to do their tasks or appearing at events before time in most cases, or on time but never late. They hate when they have something scheduled with a friend and that friend isn't punctual. They have a strict time table they might create in the morning, either mentally or have an actual checklist, and deviating from that checklist causes them to be distressed. Few scenarios showcasing people with P=3 being punctual include being first to join conference calls or reaching the conference room, ensuring no delays in doctor's appointments and ensuring they reach their before time etc.

• _Workaholic_

While being a workaholic can positively impact one's professional life, it is crucial for such individuals to recognize the importance of dedicating time to their friends and family. Constantly maintaining tight schedules without proper vacation days or breaks can lead to rifts and conflicts with loved ones. To prevent this, individuals with a P=3 should ensure they make time for social connections, take days off for self-care, utilize vacation days, and remember that a healthy work-life balance is essential for a happy and successful life.

• _Hardworking_

A hard worker is someone who devotes substantial time and effort to their tasks and goals, whether personal or professional. They are dedicated, diligent, and committed to investing significant effort and time in fulfilling their responsibilities. For example, Riya, a software engineer, consistently demonstrates her hard-working nature. She often stays late at the office to debug complex code, ensuring that projects meet tight deadlines. Despite having a busy professional life, she also commits herself to completing an online master's degree in computer science. Every evening, after finishing her work, she spends several hours studying, working on assignments, and participating in online discussions. Her dedication to both her job and her education highlights her unwavering commitment to her personal and professional growth.

• _Talk to the point_

They are honest and direct. They do not try to hide their feelings, and they are also likely to not hide their opinions either. They are direct in their approach. They value transparency in communicating with others, be it inn relationships, friendships or among family members. With this comes the fact that they are reliable, since they keep their promises and follow through their commitments. They try to avoid unnecessary drama and complexity. They confidently express their needs and desires and stand up for themselves, their beliefs, their friends and family without being aggressive about it.

- *Pampered*

Being pampered is to take care of somebody very well and make him/her feel as comfortable as possible. People with $P=3$ are given special treatment that makes them feel safe, and everyone around them give them whatever they desire. They get treated with kindness and attention, extreme and excessive care and with affection. This comes with several pros and cons as well. While the people with $P=3$ might have a habit of living in luxury, have a strong sense of support and security, have access to help and assistance whenever they need, there are times where it can go wrong as well. People with $P=3$ may become overly reliant on others and may not be able to handle challenges independently. They may even develop a sense of entitlement towards certain things and may expect special treatment in all aspects of their lives, which of course, isn't always granted. This may even affect their relationships and strain them if the other party involved feels taken for granted.

- *Loyal to the core*

Cheating on someone, i.e, to trick somebody especially if the other person trusts you, is not something people with P=3 promotes. They hate people who cheat, be it in relationships, or cheating people out of money for personal gains. They do not like to behave in a dishonest way in order to get what they want and this may even create conflicts and arguments if someone in their circle is corrupt.

PERSONALITY NUMBER 4

People born on 4, 13, 22 or 31 of any month have personality number 4.

- _Correlation with astrology_

According to astrology, number 4 is ruled by 'Rahu' or the North Node of the Moon. Rahu is considered the King of the Meteors according to the Hindu scriptures. Rahu, according to Hindu Mythology only has a head and no body, hence it influences the head region, which includes intelligence, thought process and speech of a person. It is the quality of Rahu that influences the person suddenly gaining something, be it monetary gains or fame. If Rahu enters your life, according to astrology, it may give you a lot. It may give you immense happiness, may give you monetary gains, may provide you with a happy family but also as soon as Rahu leaves your life, it may take more than it has offered. If the influences of Rahu are negative, it makes the person distracted. It makes the person make excuses for not doing their work. Rahu give people with P=4 a lot of energy and hence people with P=4 might seem to have a lot of energy. Due to its negative influences, such people are also not able to sleep early during the night, usually sleeping during the early hours of the next day. This messes with their sleep schedule, makes the person feel lethargic and be unproductive. Such people also depend on vices such as cigarettes, alcohol and in worse cases, drugs. Such people are also aggressive, always angry and irritated. They may try to lie their way out of difficult situations or may try to manipulate others into believing their version of events. They are extremely involved in mobile and technology.

- *General description*

Their imagination is good but their practical approach is weak. They know what they want to do and have brilliant ideas but they usually aren't able to put it into action without the help of others. Another trait commonly observed in people with P=4 is the fact that once they make enemies with someone, they maintain that feeling for the rest of their lives. Their motto for things relating to conflict is usually "forgive but never forget", but they also do not dish out chances to everyone. They have a limit to amount of emotional damage they let somebody do to them before completely cutting off that person from their lives. The graph of their life is usually highs and lows due to the fact that they do not have a good approach towards life. One moment they may believe that they are taking the right decisions, but as soon as the next event occurs, they regret their previous decisions, thus making even more poor decisions. They do not have stability due to these mixed thoughts and hence they might even change their jobs frequently. They are frequently also misunderstood by other people due to this behavior. They love sketching, arts and crafts, dancing etc. They get bored very easily and hence move from doing one task to another. They are unable to concentrate on one task for a very long time, which may affect them if they are students. People with P=4 do not have a tendency to open up to everyone. They ensure that they create an emotional connection that would last a long time, if not lifetime before opening up to that person. Once they open up about their feelings and general life experiences to others, they are extrovert but only in front of their friends. This is termed as 'ambivert' –

being an extrovert but only in front of specific people. They usually require a break between studies to gain more life experiences. This may happen directly after high school, before getting a bachelor's degree or right after achieving their bachelor's degree and before getting their masters degree.

- _Intelligent_

They have and show the ability to understand, learn and think. They do so very easily. They are curious, showcase strong desire to learn and explore new ideas. They ask questions and seek to understand how things work, be it how a simple ketchup is made, or how a complex machine works. They analyze given information logically and objectively. They evaluate arguments and evidences carefully before forming conclusions. They find innovative solutions to complex problems and approach challenges with creativity and resourcefulness. They quickly adjust to new situations and environments, embrace new obstacles and learn from those experiences. This also makes them make well-reasoned decisions based on evidence and logic.

- _Disciplined_

The practice of training one's mind and body so that they control their actions and obey rules. It means to carefully control the way that they work, live or behave, especially to achieve a goal. People with P=4 manage their impulsive thoughts and emotions effectively and also avoid distractions and stay focused on their tasks. They may even have a checklist to stay on top of things and to avoid missing a deadline. This comes especially handy during their college life as well as their jobs. They prioritize tasks to use time efficiently. They maintain regular routines and habits. They also take responsibility for their actions and outcomes, be it good or bad.

- *Organized*

It refers to putting or arranging things into a system or logical order. An organized person is able to plan things carefully and keep things tidy.

- *Might appear rude*

Being rude is a type of behavior that sint appropriate and usually isn't very nice. It is not having or showing concern or respect for the rights and feelings of others. People with P=4 might appear rude but in reality, they aren't. they are tough from the outside and soft from the inside, like a coconut.

- *Have lifelong friendships*

People with P=4 are someone that you connect with on a level deeper than everyone else. They maintain their friendships forever, and best believe that they try to communicate and clear any and all misunderstandings with their friends. They do not force a friendship and realize that if it has to end, it will. But they also do not give up on their friends easily. They are the "ride or die" kind of friend for everyone else. They are good listeners for their friends, always actively listening for their concerns and experiences, showing empathy and understanding without interrupting or judging. They also express their gratitude and appreciation for their friends through both small and big gestures. Their actions are such that other people are always depending on them. They prioritize spending quality time with their friends, which makes their connection stronger.

- *Extrovert*

People with P=4 are friendly people who enjoy talking to and being with other people. They thrive in group setting and feel energized by social interactions. They readily approach new people and initiate conversations. They are comfortable in both new and unfamiliar social situations due to these traits as well. They display high levels and enthusiasm. They also use body language and facial expressions to communicate effectively. They seek out new experience and enjoy exploring different environments. They also maintain a positive outlook on life and situations. They try to find the bright side in a setback, always having the attitude that even if everything is going wrong, there is something out there or some lesson or even a new experience that they might learn out of such situations.

- *Straight forward*

They are honest and avoid unnecessary politeness. However, this does not necessarily mean that they are down right rude since even thought they will put the truth out there during an argument, they also do so considering the other person's feelings. They balance directness with considering for how their words impact others. They are open about their intentions and motives in front of others and rarely hide agendas and ulterior motives. They maintain a steady and predictable behavior and hence others know where they stand with them. They are often practical and grounded in their approach to problems. They communicate their feelings or opinions in a way that is easy to understand and try to avoid ambiguous language to make sure their message is clear.

- *Anger issues*

If people with P=4 are angry, they may talk in a very strict and unkind way. They may not think over their words or the impact it may have over the other person. They say what has been on their mind for a long time without filter when they are angry, which may make others think that having an argument with people with P=4 is useless. When angry, people with P=4 do not show understanding or sympathy, which is in direct contrast to the point above. However, consideration is to be made that people with P=4 are not usually angry and are level headed people. It is a human trait to lose your wordings during anger, and it just so happens that people with P=4 may be bit harsher than others.

- *Never give up attitude*

In general, life does throw a lot of obstacles and challenges towards a person. It may be academic setbacks, financial loss, or even having a phase where a person has too many negative emotions. However, people with P=4 have such an attitude that they do not stop trying to do something. They always find motivation and comfort in the fact that if life has given them challenges, then life may also have good times planned ahead. One should always keep going no matter how things get, and with the kind of support system people with P=4 have around them, they make there comebacks.

- *Love travelling*

They are always seeking out new experiences and cultures. They never get tired of discovering the world around them. They believe that with life experiences and learning new cultures, they are only broadening their horizons for a brighter and fuller future. They live life to their fullest by such experiences. They always try to have fun and being an extrovert also comes into play with this trait.

- *Honest*

They tell the people the truth, they do not lie by omission either unless it involves other people's feelings. They are considerate about other people's feelings and hence if they have to lie by omission, they might but eventually tell that person the truth. Ey do not mislead the person in front, especially if that person is trying to pursue them romantically.

- *Multi taskers*

People with P=4 manage their time and resources effectively to handle multiple tasks simultaneously. They prioritize tasks and switch between them with ease. They keep track of various tasks and deadlines by having it marked on their calendars and creating checklists to ensure the work is done well and before time. They handle unexpected challenged without loosing focus. They avoid distractions. They remember small details and requirements for different tasks by keeping a mental note or actually jotting it down on their journals. They efficiently address issues that arise while multitasking and find creative solutions to balance multiple demands.

- *Sharp memory*

People with P=4 have sharp memory which may manifest itself as having the ability to notice the finer details that others might look over. They have a structured way of thinking which aids in better information retrieval. They are keen observers and often take mental notes of their surroundings and events. They employ techniques like spaced repetition and active recall to reinforce their memory. They often engage in activities that promote brain health such as regular physical exercise, a balanced diet and adequate sleep. They are also naturally curious and have a passion for learning which keeps their brain engaged and active.

- *Strong willpower*

They have the ability to control themselves. They have strong determination that allows them to do something difficult. They control their thoughts and behavior, especially in difficult situations. They can control their impulses and stay focused on their long term goals, even when faced with temptations or distractions. They demonstrate persistence and determination, continuing to strive towards their goals despite setbacks and difficulties. They bounce back from failures and challenges, maintaining their motivation and drive. They practice delayed gratification, i.e., postponing immediate rewards in favor of achieving more significant, long-term outcomes. they make well-considered decisions and stick to them, even when facing difficult choices.

- *Good communicators*

Communication is the act of sharing or exchanging information, ideas or feelings. They understand and respect others' perspectives and emotions, fostering trust and rapport. They communicate with self-assurance, which helps persuade and influence others positively. They use appropriate body language such as eye contact, gestures and posture to reinforce their message. They adjust their communication style based on the person they are communicating with and the context of the communication, ensuring their message is well received. They listen attentively, showing genuine interest in the speaker's message.

- *Spiritual*

They understand that life unfolds in the now, and by being fully engaged in their present experiences, they cultivate gratitude awareness and a deep sense of peace. They often exude a sense of calm and tranquility, maintaining inner peace even in stressful situations. They show deep compassion and empathy for others, often engaging in acts of kindness and understanding. They practice mindfulness, staying present in the moment and fully experiencing life as it unfolds. They also possess a strong sense of self-awareness, understanding their emotions and thoughts. They are humble, acknowledging their limitations and the interconnectedness of all life.

- *Kind hearted*

They are generous, and are willing to give other their time, resources and attention when in need without expecting anything in return. They are patient, remain calm and tolerant even in challenging situations or when dealing with difficult people. They treat everyone with respect and dignity, regardless of their status or background. They are good listeners, providing their full attention. They are quick to forgive others and do not hold grudges, understanding that everyone makes mistakes. They refrain from judging others, accepting people as they are and appreciating their unique qualities. They stand up for others, especially those who are vulnerable or marginalized, advocating for fairness and justice.

- *Visionaries*

Being a visionary means they have great plans for the future. It is the ability to think about or plan about the future with great imagination and intelligence, clear idea about what should happen or what is to be done in the future. They question existing norms and practices, looking for opportunities to innovate and improve, and are not afraid to propose bold ideas. they surround themselves with diverse individuals which helps them gain more perspective.

PERSONALITY NUMBER 5

People born on 5, 14 or 23 of any month have personality number 5.

- *Correlation with astrology*

Ruled by planet Mercury, it helps in transforming the thought process of people with P=5. Due to its influences, such people are able to make the right decisions. It also has influences on the speech of a person. If the planetary influences are negative, it makes the person have crass speech. Other negative influences include lack of savings, skin problems, short stature and tendency to harm their own child. The positive planetary influences, however, include person having a very sharp mind, being clever and extremely intelligent. They use their minds and intelligence for the right things. They have soothing speech, they talk calmly which makes them more charming in front of others as well. Such people try to find answers to several mysteries of the world and also impart their gathered knowledge. The person with positive planetary influences would look young, be good at mathematical calculations. They may love having spicy and tangy foods a lot.

- *General description*

They are extremely talkative. They would always have conversation starters ready in case they meet new people and hence do not have difficulties in making friends in new places. They have a helpful nature. They can adjust in any and all situations. They also have good support system. They cant be controlled and need some kind of freedom. They get bored very easily and hence jump from one thing to another, which is also why they are multi-talented. They always try to balance things, be it emotionally or work-life balance. They have a very good friend circle who are there for each other and take stand and back each other up as and when required. They don't like to controlled and hence don't work under anybody. Hence, a lot of people with P=5 might have their own businesses, be it big or small. They like the independence of making their own decisions and not being told what to do. They do not like physical work, they might even hate it to their core. Of course, they can't avoid physical tasks like handling their luggage when they are alone.so, they try to find ways that'll make physical tasks easier, in this case, getting a cart for their luggage, or getting a luggage bag with wheels so that they wont have to carry it around.

- *Clear speech*

It is a way of speaking in which every word, sentence and idea is spoken clearly and simply. People with P=5 focus on pronouncing words correctly. They love tongue twisters and exaggerated pronunciation drills. They speak at a moderate pace to ensure each word is clear. They develop good breath control which helps in maintaining a steady and strong voice. They incorporate pauses into their speech which gives them time to think and breathe, and also allows them to emphasize key points. They vary their tone and pitch to keep their speech interesting and engaging.

- _Luck_

It is basically to succeed or prosper as a result of chance or good fortune. A completely made up scenario to show what luck can actually do to a person's life is as follows : Akshita had always been diligent and methodical in her approach to her career, but she often felt overshadowed by colleagues who seemed to advance effortlessly. One rainy morning, while rushing to catch her usual bus, she slipped and fell, spilling her coffee. As she composed herself, a kind stranger offered her a ride to work. During the ride, they struck up a conversation, and she discovered he was the CEO of a prominent company in her industry. Impressed by her insights and passion, he invited her to an interview. Two weeks later, Akshita found herself in a new role that not only aligned perfectly with her skills but also offered opportunities she had only dreamed of. What seemed like an unfortunate accident turned into a serendipitous encounter that changed her professional trajectory, highlighting how luck can unexpectedly shape our lives.

- _Self motivated_

People with P=5 are very enthusiastic or determined to do or achieve something, without needing to be encouraged by anyone else. They keep a track of their progress and celebrate small wins along the way, which provides them with the positive reinforcement required to keep doing better. They stay positive and may use positive affirmations and focus on what they can do in a given situation rather than on the obstacle. They engage with positive and supportive people who encourage their efforts. They view failures and setbacks as learning opportunities rather than as reasons to give up. They always make it a point to analyze what went wrong and how they can improve. They maintain their physical health which also greatly influences their mental energy and motivation.

- *Family oriented*

For people with P=5, staying close to family and supporting them in their pursuits is paramount. They are always ready to help, especially with family members, as they hold blood relations in the highest regard. Prioritizing their relatives' needs above their own, individuals with P=5 offer unwavering support, whether it's financial or emotional, during tough times. They give selflessly, without expecting anything in return, fully committed to family support. However, this can sometimes lead to conflicts and tension within the family, as they may struggle to set boundaries. Their kindness and sensitivity can be exploited by some family members, potentially leading them to be treated as doormats.

- *Good communicators*

Communication involves sharing or exchanging information, ideas, or feelings. Effective communicators understand and respect others' perspectives and emotions, building trust and rapport. They communicate confidently, positively influencing and persuading others. They use suitable body language, including eye contact, gestures, and posture, to enhance their message. They adapt their communication style to suit the audience and context, ensuring their message is well-received. They also listen attentively, demonstrating genuine interest in what the speaker is saying.

- *Moody*

People with P=5 often change their moods in a way that other people cannot predict. Their mood changes suddenly, they may become extremely angry one moment and forget all about the anger and the cause of anger a few hours later, and become sad instead. They are highly sensitive to their own emotions and those of others. Their moods may oscillate between periods of happiness, irritability, sadness or anger without an apparent cause. They may struggle to manage their emotions, leading to outbursts or emotional reactions that may seem disproportionate to their situations. During periods of low mood, they may withdraw from social interactions and prefer solitude, seeking space to process their emotions privately. They may be more reactive to external stimuli, such as noise, stress, or changes in their environment, which can exacerbate their mood fluctuations.

- *Bounce back easily*

These people are resilient individuals who maintain a positive outlook, believing in their ability to overcome challenges and find solutions. They are flexible and are able to adjust their strategies or mindset in response to changing circumstances. They are resourceful and proactive in finding solutions to problems, focusing on what they can control rather than what they cant. They have a strong support network of friends, family or mentors who provide them encouragement, guidance and practical assistance. They are able to find humor in difficult situations, which can help alleviate stress and provide perspective.

- *Free bird*

People with P=5 are free birds. They love being independent and strive on seeking a balance between freedom and responsibility, recognizing that true freedom comes from making conscious choices and taking ownership of the consequences. They are authentic and true to themselves, refusing to compromise their values or integrity for the sake of conformity. They express themselves openly and freely, whether through creative outlets, personal style or their way of life. They prioritize their time and energy on activities and relationships that align with their values and bring them joy and fulfillment.

- *Philanthropist*

Philanthropist is someone who freely gives money and help to people who need it. It is a person who donates time, money, experience, skills or talent to help create a better world. Their primary aim is to improve the quality of life for others and address societal issues. They often develop well thought-out plans for their donations, targeting specific issues or communities to maximize impact. They may support a wide range of cause including but not limited to education, healthcare, the environment, poverty alleviation, arts and culture etc. they actively engage with the causes they support, often serving on boards, volunteering, or participating in fundraising efforts. They may collaborate with other philanthropists, non profits and governmental organizations to leverage their impact and avoid duplication of efforts.

- *Emotionally stable*

Maintaining emotional stability involves developing habits and practices that help people with P=5 manage their emotions effectively, cope with stress and maintain a balanced outlook on life. They regularly reflect on their emotions and what triggers them. They practice observing their own emotions without being overwhelmed by them. They maintain a healthy lifestyle with regular exercise, a balanced diet and adequate sleep/ they develop effective stress management techniques such as deep breathing exercises, yoga or engaging in hobbies that relax them. They constantly try to pursue activities and hobbies that bring them joy and fulfillment. They are kind to themselves, especially during difficult times. They acknowledge the fact that their efforts were worth it regardless of the outcome, and that it is okay to make mistakes.

- *Happy go lucky*

People with P=5 are carefree, optimistic and have a positive outlook on life. They don't stress over small problems or worry excessively about their future, choosing to focus and live in the present. They bounce back quickly from setbacks and difficulties, not letting the negative experiences weigh them down for too long. They are usually outgoing and enjoy social interactions, making friends easily and spreading positivity in their social circles. They tend to manage stress well, often using humor and relaxation techniques to keep their stress levels in check. They are content with their own lives and do not feel envious of others' success or possessions. They often inspire and uplift those around them, creating a positive and encouraging environment.

- *Smart workers*

People with P=5 possess practical intelligence and resourcefulness, enabling them to navigate and thrive in everyday situations. They can quickly assess a situation and find effective solutions using available resources. They are adept at making the most of what they have, often finding creative and unconventional ways to get things done. They are skilled negotiators and are able to persuade others and find mutually beneficial solutions. They have a keen ability to evaluate risk and benefit ratio, making calculated decisions to avoid potential dangers. They often use humor and charm to diffuse tension and build positive relationships.

- *Good advisors*

Becoming a good advisor requires a combination of knowledge, empathy, communication skills and commitment to well-being of those one advises. People with P=5 establish a foundation of trust through honesty, reliability and confidentiality. They ensure that those they advise feel safe in sharing their issues and challenges with them. They convey their advice clearly and concisely. They avoid jargon and ensure that their explanations are easy to understand. They provide unbiased and objective advice by avoiding letting personal biases or emotions influence it.

CHAPTER SEVEN

PERSONALITY NUMBER 6

People born on 6, 15 or 24 of any month have personality number 6.

- *Correlation with astrology*

According to astrology, number 6 is ruled by the planet Venus, which is quiet beautiful. People with P=6 are extremely bright people. Others may call them the "sunshine" of the group since they have a very pleasing personality. They are happy-go-lucky people, and try to make others happy as well. One thing is for sure that they will not meet their friends with a dull face. The planet influences the person's personality and makes them friendly. Such people are also extremely talented in their fields of work. They have good handwork. Influences on the face include people having dimples on their chins or cheeks, having round face frames till their jawlines etc. the planet Venus is related to things like love, family, children, property, happiness, marriage, skills, vehicles etc. if the planetary influences are positive then the person with P=6 will be charming, provide the person with fame, success and fame. If the planetary influences are negative then the person with P=6 would be having financial problems, marriage problems and may even have problems with their children – whether it be with conceiving the child, having issues with the child's health or having tense relation with their children.

- *General description*

They have strong feelings and faith for God in general and believe with all their heart in their religion. It helps them cope with difficulties in their lives. One thing about people with P=6 is that their lives are not smooth after marriage. It might be due to general miscommunications with their partners or having feelings of frustrations about their children, but they might feel as if they have lost their old selves, their old personalities after their marriage.

- *Beautiful*

A beautiful person, in the most holistic sense, embodies qualities that go beyond physical appearance. Their beauty radiates from a combination of their character, actions and demeanor. They are kind and compassionate, show empathy and consideration for others and often go out of their way to help those in need. They are true to themselves and others, displaying honesty and integrity. They believe in themselves and their abilities without arrogance, inspiring others through their self-assuredness. Despite their strengths and accomplishments, they remain humble and are able to recognize their own limitations and appreciate the contributions of others.

- *Magnetic aura*

One might say a person has a magnetic aura when they possess a captivating and charismatic presence that draws others to them. People with P=6 exude an intangible quality that makes them highly attractive, influential or intriguing to those around them. Such people often have a combination of traits such as confidence, charm, authenticity and warmth that naturally captivate others' attention and leave a lasting impression. Their energy and charisma seem to have a magnetic effect, effortlessly attracting others and leaving them feeling inspired, uplifted or deeply connected in their presence.

- *Family oriented*

People with P=6 are extremely family oriented and this may manifest as valuing and preserving their family's history, traditions and cultural heritage, passing down stories, values and heirlooms to future generations. They are willing to make sacrifices and compromises for the well-being of their family, they express love, affection and concern for their family members openly, creating an emotionally supportive and nurturing environment. They actively participate in family responsibilities and duties, whether its caregiving, household chores or financial support. They celebrate achievements and milestones of their family members, showing pride and enthusiasm for their success.

- *Multitasker*

Individuals characterized by P=4 exhibit adept time and resource management skills, allowing them to navigate numerous tasks concurrently. They adeptly prioritize assignments, seamlessly transitioning between them as needed. Employing calendars and checklists, they meticulously track deadlines, ensuring timely completion of tasks to a high standard. When confronted with unforeseen challenges, they maintain focus without faltering, actively avoiding distractions. Their capacity to recall intricate task details, whether mentally noted or documented in journals, enhances their multitasking proficiency. They adeptly troubleshoot emerging issues while multitasking, employing innovative approaches to harmonize diverse demands.

- *Talkative*

They like to talk a lot. They are friendly, open and willing to communicate with strangers. They are often skilled at building rapport and establishing connections through conversation. They may struggle with active listening skills as their enthusiasm for speaking can sometimes overshadow their ability to attentively listen to others. In group settings they may dominate the conversation, speaking more frequently and for longer durations when compared to others. They may also freely share personal details about themselves, including their interests, experiences and emotions as a way of connecting with others. They may find pauses or lulls in conversations uncomfortable and may actively seek to fill these gaps with additional dialogue.

- *Attractive accent*

There are many things that contribute to the attractiveness of a speech than just the content. Good speakers italicize their words properly, even though they are saying something ordinary, they know which words to put stress on so that they have a greater impact. People with P=6 have accents characterized by melodic or rhythmic quality in their pronunciation, which listeners may find pleasing and captivating. They may add an element of novelty to the conversation. Accents are associated with sophistication, intelligence or cultural richness, which may be perceives as attractive due to positive associations they evoke.

- *Charming personality*

Having a charming personality entails possessing a combination of qualities and behaviors that consistently attract and captivate others. People with P=6 greet others with genuine warmth and friendliness, making others feel instantly comfortable and welcomed in their presence. They exude self-assurance and confidence which can be magnetic to others. They are adept at communication, using humor, wit and charm to engage and captivate those around them. They possess social grace and tact, navigating social situations with ease and making others feel respected and appreciated.

- *Will power*

People with P=6 possess self-regulation skills, exhibiting strong resolve in tackling challenging tasks. They manage their thoughts and actions adeptly, particularly in adverse circumstances. They exercise restraint over their impulses, remaining committed to their overarching objectives, even amidst allurements or diversions. They exhibit perseverance and tenacity, persisting in their pursuits despite encountering obstacles and setbacks. They recover swiftly from setbacks and adversities, sustaining their enthusiasm and determination. They embrace delayed gratification, opting to defer instant gratifications in pursuit of greater, enduring achievements.

- *Travelers*

People with P=6 have natural curiosity and thirst for exploring new places, cultures and experiences. They seek to broaden their horizons and gain a deeper understanding of the world. It offers them an opportunity for adventure and excitement, whether its trying new activities, exploring natural wonders or embarking on spontaneous journeys. They often may also plan travel destinations rich in historical significance, landmarks and monuments. They find inspiration and creativity in new environments, cultures and experiences. They return from their travels with fresh perspectives, ideas and insights to duel their creative endeavors.

- *Foodie*

People with P=6 have ardent or refined interest in good and they eat food not only out of hunger but also as a hobby. They view food as a means of socializing and connecting with others. They value food as a cultural expression and reflection of history, tradition and identity. They enjoy learning about the culinary heritage of different regions and communities. They might be passionate home cooks who enjoy experimenting with recipes, ingredients and cooking methods.

- *Attract luxury*

They enjoy expensive and beautiful things. They enjoy comfort. They like expensive things that are pleasant to have but is not really a necessary. They expect excellence and hence prioritize craftsmanship, materials and attention to detail.

- *Cleanliness*

People with P=6 are particular about having clean surroundings. They set aside time each day for basic cleaning tasks such as making bed, doing the dishes, wiping countertops and tidying up the clutter. They declutter regularly, getting rid of items that they no longer need or use. They may stock upon cleaning essentials such as all-purpose cleaners, disinfectants, microfiber cloths, sponges etc and may go and research in-depth about products that are safe and effective for surfaces they are cleaning. They may also hire professionals to clean articles such as carpets or to get certain areas of their homes clean.

- *Post marriage challenges*

People with P=6 may experience difficulty in effectively communicating their needs, desires and concerns to each other which may lead to misunderstanding, conflicts and resentment if not addressed. They may often find it hard to adjust with their partners, often in small matters such as division of household chores. Financial matters can be a source of stress for the couple especially if they have different spending habits than their partner, different financial goals or attitude towards money. They may not be able to balance relationships with their in-laws and extended family members and conflicts may arise over boundaries, expectations and differing family dynamics. All this being said, if people with P=6 only communicate with their partners effectively, finding common ground and establishing clear boundaries, they may not have as many challenges post marriage and they might even get resolved entirely.

- *Romantic*

People with P=6 believe in the power of importance of love as driving force in life. They often view love as transformative and transcendent experience that enrich their lives. They have a keen eye for beauty in all its forms, whether its found in nature, art, music, literature or human relationships. They tend to be idealistic in their outlook, often envisioning an idealized version of love and relationships. They have high expectations for romance and strive to create romantic experiences that align with their ideals.

- *Confident*

It is basically feeling or showing that one is sure about their abilities and opinions. People with P=6 trust in their own judgement, decision and abilities. They have a positive self image and a healthy sense of self worth. They accept themselves for who they are, flaws and all, and do not seek validation or approval from others to feel good about themselves. They are resilient in face of challenges and setbacks. They are assertive in their needs, boundaries and opinions but in a respectful manner.

- *Creative*

To be creative entails possessing the capacity to generate novel concepts or produce original works. Creatives exhibit a readiness to delve into fresh ideas, viewpoints, and potentials, embracing unconventional modes of thought. They manifest a keen thirst for knowledge, eagerly delving into diverse subjects, curiosities, and encounters, frequently posing insightful inquiries and seeking varied wellsprings of inspiration. Their expressions convey distinctive and inventive perspectives, methods, and understandings, showcasing a personalized flair and imaginative essence.

- *Never give up attitude*

Life often presents individuals with numerous obstacles and challenges. These may include academic setbacks, financial losses, or periods filled with overwhelming negative emotions. However, people with a P=6 mindset possess an attitude that drives them to keep striving, no matter the circumstances. They draw motivation and comfort from the belief that if life can bring challenges, it can also bring good times in the future. This perspective encourages them to persist regardless of the difficulties they encounter. Additionally, the robust support system surrounding those with a P=6 mindset plays a crucial role in their ability to rebound. With the encouragement and assistance of their friends, family, and mentors, they are able to overcome setbacks and make strong comebacks. Ultimately, their positive outlook and the support they receive empower them to continue moving forward, confident that better days lie ahead. This resilience is a testament to the strength of the P=6 mindset, proving that with determination and a solid support network, one can overcome any challenge life presents.

- *Believer of spiritual laws of universe*

The concept of spiritual laws of universe is often associated with philosophical or metaphysical principles that guide human consciousness and spiritual growth. People with P=6 may believe in spiritual laws of universe such as the law of attraction, which states that posits that like attracts like, suggesting that the energy you put out into the universe whether positive or negative will be returned to you. It emphasizes the power of thoughts, beliefs and intentions in shaping one's reality. They may also believe in other laws such as the law of karma, law of vibration, law of detachment, law of intention etc.

- *Extrovert*

Individuals with P=6 are sociable and enjoy engaging with others in social settings. They thrive in group environments and find social interactions energizing. They are proactive in initiating conversations and are at ease in unfamiliar social contexts. Their outgoing nature is complemented by their enthusiasm and expressive communication style, utilizing body language and facial expressions effectively. They are adventurous and open to new experiences, relishing the opportunity to explore diverse environments. Maintaining a positive perspective, they approach setbacks with optimism, recognizing the potential for growth, learning, or new experiences even in challenging situations.

CHAPTER EIGHT

PERSONALITY NUMBER 7

People born on 7, 16 or 25 of any month have personality number 7.

- _Correlation with astrology_

Governed by the "Ketu" or the South Node of the Moon. It gives the people with P=7 incredible intuition power. It isn't as bad a "Rahu" or the North Node of the Moon. Ketu makes the person spiritual. A student being governed by Ketu can basically look at a book, read it once or twice and understand the material with little to no difficulty. They remember the life lessons from their previous lives, which can also be interpreted as their soul's lessons. People with P=7 should believe their inner monologue since it is probably their soul having learnt that lesson trying to guide them in the right direction. If there are negative influences of the South Node, the person would have poor concentration. This may make the person lose focus very easily, may not let a student with P=7 study properly and it may also make the person day dream about unnecessary scenarios that may not even happen.

- *General description*

People with P=7 have a lot of knowledge, be it academic or about life or even just random facts. Such people love to gain more knowledge and also love to share their knowledge with their peers. They have a very deep connection with people having P=4. People with P=7 stay connected with P=4 for a long time, only slightly diminishing contact due to life. However, one slightly negative point about people with P=7 is the fact that they never admit their mistakes. They would never apologize for their mistake if they don't see their actions as being wrong. They would justify their feelings by presenting facts in front of the person they are arguing with, only apologizing if they realize it themselves that their actions and words may have seriously hurt the person in front of them. They are extremely attached to their mothers and can share almost anything with them. They have a very good sense of fashion.

- *Satisfaction with life*

Life satisfaction refers to an individual's overall feelings about their life. It involves cultivating a sense of fulfillment, contentment and purpose. People with P=7 take time to reflect on what truly matters to them and what they value most in their lives. They clarify their priorities to help them make decisions that align with their authentic selves. They identify goals that are meaningful to them whether it is related to their careers, personal growth or other aspects of life.

- *Spiritual*

They recognize the importance of living in the present moment, embracing each experience with gratitude and awareness to foster a profound sense of serenity. Even amidst challenges, they radiate a peaceful demeanor, demonstrating inner calm and resilience. They extend genuine compassion and empathy to others, frequently demonstrating kindness and empathy in their interactions. By practicing mindfulness, they remain grounded in the present moment, fully embracing the richness of life as it unfolds. Additionally, they exhibit a keen self-awareness, attuned to their emotions and thoughts, and humbly acknowledge their own limitations while appreciating the interconnectedness of all living beings.

- *Knowledgeable*

People with P=7 are able to apply their knowledge effectively to solve problems, make informed decisions and achieve goals. They demonstrate practical wisdom and resourcefulness in real-world situations. They are aware of the limit of their knowledge and expertise and recognize when they don't know something and are willing to seek out that additional information to fill gaps in their knowledge. They approach learning with humility, recognizing that there is always more to learn and that knowledge is constantly evolving. They are open to feedback and constructive criticism and value the perspectives and expertise of others.

- *Humble*

Being humble involves having a modest and unpretentious attitude, acknowledging one's limitations and showing respect and appreciation for others. People with P=7 cultivate a mindset of gratitude by regularly acknowledging and appreciating the people, experiences and blessings in their lives. They practice active listening by giving others their full attention and genuinely seeking to understand their perspectives, opinions and experiences. They resist the urge to interrupt ro dominate conversations and show respect for others' view points. They refrain from seeking attention or validation through boasting or bragging about their accomplishments, possessions or talents. They instead let their actions speak for themselves and allow others to recognize their achievements organically.

- _Down to earth_

People with P=7 remain humble and unassuming despite their achievements or status. They are approachable, friendly and genuine in their interactions with others and don't put on airs or act superior, making others feel comfortable around them. They lead a modest lifestyle and are content with simple pleasures of life, they are not overly materialistic or concerned with superficial possessions. They show kindness, empathy and a willingness to help others without expecting anything in return. They prioritize human connection and relationships over personal gain.

- _Ups and downs in life_

A mixture of good and bad things happen to people with P=7. They acknowledge that life is not always smooth or easy and that people encounter both positive and negative outcomes. They believe in the notion that challenges and setbacks are a natural part of human experience but that they are also often followed by better times. With the comfort of such thought, and the amazing support they gain from their family and friends, they go through the most challenging of times.

- _Intelligent_

They possess and demonstrate a keen aptitude for comprehension, learning, and critical thinking, effortlessly engaging in these processes. They exhibit curiosity and a fervent eagerness to acquire knowledge, actively seeking to explore novel ideas and concepts. Whether unraveling the intricacies of everyday items like schezwan sauce or deciphering the workings of intricate machinery, they exhibit a penchant for inquiry and understanding. They methodically analyze information with a logical and objective approach, meticulously evaluating arguments and evidence prior to drawing conclusions. When confronted with complex challenges, they exhibit ingenuity and resourcefulness, devising innovative solutions to overcome obstacles. Adaptable to new circumstances and environments, they embrace challenges as opportunities for growth, learning, and adaptation. Their ability to synthesize information and apply logical reasoning enables them to make well-founded decisions based on evidence and sound judgment.

- *Researcher*

Researchers possess a combination of skills, qualities and traits that enable them to conduct scholarly enquiry, analyze data and contribute to advancement of knowledge in their field. They are naturally curious individuals who possess a strong desire to explore, investigate and understand the world around them. They engage in rigorous critical thinking, carefully evaluating evidence, arguments and assumptions. They are skilled at analyzing and interpreting complex data sets, research findings and scholarly literature.

- *Strong intuition*

People with P=7 are able to make decisions based on gut feelings or inner knowing. They are often highly sensitive to subtle cues, energies and vibrations in their environment. They may pick up on emotions, atmospheres or non verbal communication signals that others overlook. They have a deep trust in their inner wisdom and intuition. They rely on their gut feelings, instincts, and inner knowing to guide them in decision-making and problem solving processes. They approach life with an open mind and a willingness to explore unconventional ideas, possibilities and perspectives. They are empathetic and compassionate towards others, tuning into the emotions and experiences of those around them.

- *Sensitive*

People with P=7 are acutely aware of their emotions and those of others, often experiencing feelings intensely and being attuned to subtle emotional cues. They are vulnerable to criticism, rejection or perceived slights, leading them to be more cautious or guarded in their interactions with others. They possess a rich inner world and a strong creative drive, channeling their emotions and experiences into artistic expression, writing or tother creative pursuits. They may become easily overwhelmed by external stimuli such as loud noises, bright lights or crowded environments, leading them to seek solitude or quiet spaces too recharge.

- *Calm*

They are emotionally stable and resilient. They possess patience and tolerance, allowing them to navigate through life's ups and downs with grace and composure. They are skilled communicators who can express themselves clearly and assertively without resorting to anger or aggression. They respect their own boundaries as well as those of others. They are assertively able to communicate their needs and preferences without becoming confrontational or defensive. They are able to regulate their emotions effectively and make conscious choices about how to respond to different situations.

- *Positive aura*

They have a positive outlook on life, focusing on opportunities and possibilities rather than dwelling on challenges or setbacks. They see the silver lining in difficult situations and maintain hope for the future. They express gratitude for the blessings in their life and appreciate the small joys and pleasures that each day brings. They show appreciation for the people and the experiences that enrich their lives. They go out of their way to help others and make a positive difference in the lives of those around them. They are genuine and authentic in their interactions with others, being true to themselves and not pretending to be someone they're not. They are comfortable in their own skin and embrace their unique qualities and quirks.

- *Counselors*

Counselors possess blend of skills and qualities that enable them to provide effective guidance, support and assistance to individuals seeking help. They are empathetic and compassionate individuals who understand and resonate with feelings, experiences and struggles of the person in front. They create a safe and supportive environment where the others feel heard, validates and understood. They pay close attention to verbal and nonverbal communication cues and demonstrate respect and interest in others' concerns, allowing them to build rapport and trust.

- *Motivators*

A motivator is someone who inspires and encourages others to achieve their goals, overcome obstacles and fulfill their potential. They are passionate about their own goals and aspirations and this passion is contagious. They soeak with enthusiasm and conviction, igniting a fire within others to pursue their dreams with fervor. They have a clear vision of what they want to achieve and are able to communicate this vision in a way that inspires others to take action. They demonstrate resilience in the face of adversity, bouncing back from setbacks and failures with determination and perseverance.

- *Wise*

People with P=7 have a profound understanding of themselves, others and the world around them through life experiences, self reflection and learning from others. They approach life with an open mind and a willingness to consider different perspectives, ideas and beliefs. They have high level of emotional intelligence, enabling them to understand and manage their own emotions effectively, as well as empathize with the feelings and experiences of others. They have a patient and tolerant demeanor, able to remain calm and composed in difficult situations. They possess strong morals and ethics.

CHAPTER NINE

PERSONALITY NUMBER 8

People born on 8, 17 or 26 of any month have personality number 8.

- *Correlation with astrology*

P=8 is governed by the planet Saturn according to astrology. People with P=8 have the same hairstyle almost throughout the entirety of their lifetime. Such people are also actively trying to seek out the truth and hence try to dig up facts to get to the truth, even though it might end up hurting them. If influences of the planet Saturn are bad, the person would become extremely mysterious. They would try to act and behave in "intelligent" ways. They try to overthink situations that are not even happening around them. They might have a tendency to misunderstand situations to extreme levels. This makes them scrutinize every action of other people, which may even hurt their family in the long run. Other negative influences of Saturn on people with P=8 include them having dead skin, high anxiety levels, ego problems, arguments with their loved ones etc. On the other hand, if the influence of the planet is positive, the person would not have a lot of movement. They would mostly sit idle and may listen to other's point of views. Other positive influences include person loving technology and being "tech savvy", balanced in their finances, emotions, physical health and life in general.

- *General description*

Such people are unable to completely express themselves. They find it extremely hard to say what they are feeling out loud even though they have completely comprehended their feelings about a situation. This also includes them not being romantic towards their partners or them not showcasing gestures to make their partners feel secure. Do they deeply appreciate their partners and want to make them feel special? Absolutely, yet they do not know how to do it. They might show their love in smaller gestures such as sending their partners food when they are sick, ensuring they take their medicines on time etc but they do not know how to make grand gestures. They are extremely kind hearted and believe in acts of service as their love language rather than other things. They are extremely generous as well, whether it be with their close ones or a complete stranger. Such people are usually extremely active in their old age as well.

- *Fighters*

People with P=8 are resilient and have the ability to bounce back from setbacks, failures and hardships. They view obstacles as opportunities to grow and learn. They have unwavering commitment to their goals and a strong will to success. Their determination fuels their persistence and effort. They exhibit bravery in the face of fear and danger. They are willing to take risks and confront difficult situations head on, showing both physical and mental courage. They have high level of self-discipline and control. Their perseverance is a key factor in their ability to ultimately succeed.

- *Lots of struggles*

Struggles are a natural part of life and can arise in various contexts, each presenting unique challenges and requiring different coping strategies. These struggles may be financial due to unexpected expenses, debt or employment, health struggles, relationship struggles, career struggles etc.

- *Hard working*

People with P=7 set clear goals and remain committed to achieving them. They are dependable and can be counted on to complete tasks on time. They maintain a steady level of effort and performance over time. They have genuine interest and enthusiasm for their work. They effectively prioritize tasks to ensure that the most important and urgent ones are completed. They handle stress well and do not let it affect their productivity. They pay close attention to details and ensure that their work is accurate and of high quality.

- *Adventurous*

People with P=7 have a deep appreciation for the beauty and excitement of the world around them. They possess the stamina to undertake physically demanding adventures. They are often able to maintain high level of physical fitness to support their adventurous activities. They appreciate and respect different cultures and perspectives. Through gaining such vast experiences and view points, they are able to think outside the box and find creative solutions to problems.

- *Workaholic*

They frequently have long working hours, beyond what is required or expected. They find it difficult to disconnect from work and may constantly check emails, take work-related calls or think about work even during leisure time or personal activities. The constant focus on work can lead to chronic stress and may lead to people with P=8 feel overwhelmed, anxious and pressured by their workloads and deadlines. They often neglect their personal life including family, friends, hobbies and self care. They have trouble delegating tasks to others and believe that only they can do the job correctly, leading to an overwhelming workload.

- *Good things delay*

Even though they work really hard or put their 110% into completing their tasks efficiently and perfectly, they might not get rewards for it. It is often observed that people with P=8 get their rewards later. Much after the completion of their work and may be explained by planetary influences according to Hindu scriptures.

- *Family oriented*

People with P=8 have natural inclination to nurture and care for their environment for their family members, providing a loving and supportive home environment. They value and actively participate in family celebrations, holidays and special occasions, creating and cherishing shared memories. They are skilled at managing and resolving conflicts within the family. They take an active interest in the lives of their family members, participating in their activities, celebrations and milestones and offering guidance and support. They uphold and pass down family values, traditions and cultural practices, emphasizing the importance of heritage and shared history.

- *Strict and disciplined*

People with P=8 consistently enforce rules and maintain high standards in both personal and professional life, showing little tolerance for deviations. They are always on time for appointments, meeting and deadlines, valuing time management and expecting same from others. They set clear boundaries and expectations, both for themselves and for those around them. They hold themselves and others accountable for their actions and responsibilities, emphasizing the importance of reliability and integrity. They show respect for authority and established protocols, expecting the same respect from others.

- *Organized*

They keep their physical and digital spaces clean and free of clutter. They organize their belongings in a logical manner, making it easy to find what they need. They avoid procrastination by sticking to their plans and schedules. They keep detailed records and documentation for reference and accountability. They can adjust their plans and strategies when unexpected changes occur. They regularly monitor their progress and make adjustments as needed to stay on track.

- *Work not appreciated*

Regardless of how much they do for other people, they are often underappreciated. Regardless of the hours people with P=8 put in, or the resources, or the physical and emotional efforts, they should accept the fact that they aren't going to be appreciated by other people. It is in their best interest to not make others see their true worth or they would be the one seen as someone who does favors and also makes others feel guilty about putting them through so much hard work.

- *Believe on their own practical experience*

People with P=8 believe that even though other people have gained experience by going through similar situations as them, it is in their best interest to keep their own experience and learn everything themselves rather than gaining insights from other people. They believe that others' experiences would be tangled with their biases and hence would not allow them to gain the life lesson they are supposed to. They also believe that everyone has a different background, different nature and hence would rather like to self evaluate their reactions to a particular situation.

- *Follow ethics*

People with P=8 demonstrate integrity by being honest, trustworthy and consistent in their actions and decisions. They are transparent in their communication, avoiding deception, lies and exaggeration. They take accountability for their actions and decisions. They treat everyone fairly and impartially, ensuring that their decisions and actions are just and equitable.

- *Devoted to their countries*

People with P=8 are patriotic and support and love their country even when its going through rough or difficult times.

- *Good management skills*

They are effective managers who are able to demonstrate strong leadership qualities and inspire and motivate others to achieve common goals. They possess excellent communication skills both verbal and written, enabling them to articulate ideas clearly, lsten actively and provide constructive feedback. They are adept at making informed and timely decisions, weighing options, analyzing risks and considering the needs and perspectives of stakeholders. They understand importance of delegation and empower team members by assigning tasks and responsibilities according to individual strengths and abilities. They excel in organization and planning, efficiently allocating resources, setting priorities and coordinating tasks to meet deadlines and objectives.

PERSONALITY NUMBER 9

People born on 9, 18 or 27 of any month have personality number 9.

- *Correlation with astrology*

People with P=9, according to astrology, are governed by the planet Mars, which is blood red in color. This denotes action and energy. Influences on the face includes copper-coloured undertone. The complexion may be pale-coloured, or brown-coloured, or even black-coloured but the undertone is copper. Other influences of Mars on the body structure include tall height and slightly curvy. The person is self confident, brave and daring. Person would also have dense bone structure as well as good blood circulation. If influences of the planet Mars are negative, the person would have extreme anger issues. They would be very egoistic. Getting small injuries would be a regular occurrence and they might have weak bones as well if influences of Mars are negative.

- *General description*

People with P=9 are angry, as discussed and hence are always ready to fight. They do not take disrespect lightly, nor are they able to handle criticism or jokes and jabs. They take everything personally, and hence when angry, may be ready to have arguments or even physically fight.

Such people also are not ready to leave their work incomplete. Best believe them to complete their work during late hours of the night or early hours of the morning if they have an upcoming deadline.

Such people are also multitalented, with many impressive skills to impress others. Since they cannot take criticism themselves, they also do not like to pass their judgement or criticize other's work. Such people are good at physical work such as building stuff from scratch, DIY projects etc. such people are also stubborn for their goal, and would do anything to achieve it. Since they are multitalented, they are also extremely open to learn more things, be it hobbies, languages, skills etc. they have good fashion sense. They are courageous and adventurous.

- _Energetic and full of energy_

They are full of energy and need to be enthusiastic. It is one of those engrained traits of people with P=9 that they are energetic and also somehow have such a radiating aura that people in their company automatically become energetic. The people with P=9 are always active and never get tired. They like doing activities during their personal time which may include hiking, doing volunteering activities such as helping in local shelters, participating in community clean-up events, organizing entertainment nights with family and friends etc.

- _Aggressive_

Being aggressive basically means showing anger and a willingness to attack other people. Aggression is generally considered a behavior that is intended to cause physical or psychological harm to another. Violence refers to a more extreme form to aggression. People with P=2 are someone who may be considered "dominating", given that they try to manipulate or control others in work environments or even in personal relationships. They may use harsh, blunt or hurtful words during arguments which they might not even realize that it'll hurt the person in front. People with P=9 are known to hold grudges over small things and try to seek revenge from their enemies. They might even take pleasure in watching their rival fail or come across misfortune.

- *Egoistic*

People with P=9 are often considered egoistic since they focus primarily on their own needs and desires. They often disregard feelings of others. They lack empathy and struggle to understand other people's perspective. They insist on having their way and are reluctant to consider other people's point of views. They have a habit of quickly dismissing other's contributions, often belittling it in front of an audience. When confronted about such behavior, people with P=9 avoid taking responsibilities for their mistakes and blame others for their own shortcomings or failures.

- *Moody*

It refers to often changing moods in a way that people cannot predict. Their feelings and behaviors change frequently and in particular they become depressed or angry without any warnings.

- *Always want to win*

They want to be the best in whatever field they are in. they want to stand first in competitions, want to complete given tasks before time to gain credits of being reliable etc.

- *Leaders*

Being a leader, people with P=9 have the abilities or strengths shown particularly by those in management roles. They aid in guiding and encouraging a group of people or their team towards achieving a common goal or a set of goals. Their skill sets include communication, negotiation, conflict resolution, decision making and more.

- *Fighting spirit*

It is the mental state in which person is prepared to cope with a challenging situation and does not shy away from the difficulties they face, even when the odds are against them.

- *Don't criticize*

Criticism is basically to say what is bad or wrong with somebody/something. People with P=9 do not have a tendency to tell people what they have done wrong or what opinion they have about their decisions unless it affects their work / job. With this comes the trait that they also do not like to take criticism about their work. They do not like the fact that others are observing their work up close and personal, or that they are closely watching their pattern of decision making and behaviors enough to tell them what is right and what is wrong.

- *Never give up attitude*

It is a powerful and motivating phrase that encourages perseverance, resilience and determination in the face of challenges, setbacks or obstacles. People with P=9 try standing up and repeating their task one more time, even if they feel that they wont be able to complete the task or feel like quitting

- *Stubborn*

People with P=9 are resistant to change and prefer to stick to their established ways of thinking and behaving. They are not easily swayed by opinions or suggestions of others. They are independent and assertive. They have limited perspective and are unwilling to consider alternative viewpoints or new information. They become defensive when challenged or criticized, reacting emotionally rather than rationally. They may avoid situations where they feel vulnerable or exposed, preferring to maintain a façade of strength and certainty. Their stubbornness can lead to conflicts and strained relationships with other. Others may find it challenging to connect with them or may avoid engaging with them altogether.

- *Humanitarian*

A humanitarian is someone who demonstrates a deep commitment to promoting human welfare and alleviating suffering, often through acts of compassion, generosity and advocacy. They prioritize the well being and interests of other above their own, often sacrificing personal gain or comfort to help those in need. They are driven by a desire to serve and make a positive difference in the lives of others. They empower individuals and communities to become self-sufficient and resilient, providing them with tools and knowledge and support needed to overcome challenges and build better futures.

About The Author

Shalu Singh is an acclaimed numerologist, known for her successful client service. With a background in numerology, future predictions and teaching, Shalu brings a wealth of knowledge and experience to her latest book on the basics of Numerology.

Born in Jaipur, Shalu developed an interest in numerology in 2020, particularly in how numbers shape our future and even affect our day to day lives.

In addition to her academic and client service, Shalu has been actively involved in education and delivers lectures for school students at local tuition. Her passion for making education accessible to a broader audience is evident in her writing, where she strives to educate and inspire her readers by weaving compelling narratives from real life cases.

When not writing, Shalu enjoys traveling, and spending time with her family. She resides in New Delhi with her husband.

Connect with me:

Phone no. - 9891913150
Mail ID - shaludv28s@gmail.com

Thank You

As I celebrate the completion and release of "Number's Magic - A guide to numerology"., I wanted to take a moment to express my deepest gratitude to all of you who have been a part of this journey.

Your unwavering support and encouragement have been a constant source of motivation for me. Writing this book has been a labour of love, and knowing that I had such a wonderful community cheering me on made all the difference. Your kind words, thoughtful feedback, and enthusiastic anticipation have been truly inspiring.

I am incredibly grateful to each and every one of you for believing in me and my work. Your support has not only fuelled my creativity but has also given me the strength to persevere through the challenges of the writing process.

Thank you for being a part of this journey with me. I hope my book brings you as much joy and inspiration as you have given me.

www.ingramcontent.com/pod-product-compliance
Lightning Source LLC
Chambersburg PA
CBHW031325130726
47988CB00007B/2983